SOME HAGGIS TALES

By

R.A. MacKenzie

With Sketches By

Gillian MacKenzie

THE TROUSER PRESS

To all
Meat Products
everywhere.

Published by

THE TROUSER PRESS

Isle of Mull

© Text R.A. MacKenzie 1992

© Illustrations Gillian MacKenzie 1992

ISBN 1 872908 02 0

Trade distribution

clan books

Doune

All rights reserved. No part of this publication
may be reproduced or boiled with turnips without
the prior permission of the publisher.

Printed by
PDC Copyprint, Glasgow

The Haggis Go To Mull

In the very early days
When Haggis were so few,
Often they were at a loss
In knowing what to do.

One little band of Haggis men
Lived in Ardnamurchan.
Their leader was a happy chap,
Who always wore a turban.

Cheerfully he said one day,
'In looking o'er the water,
I've seen a Haggis over there.
What's more, he has a daughter!'

He had, of course, spent all the day,
In his Observatory,
Looking out across the Sound,
Right into Tobermory.

They built themselves a wooden raft,
And launched it on the waters.
A few feet out it promptly sank.
The Chief lost some supporters.

The Haggis are a toughish lot,
Not easily deterred,
They built themselves a proper boat,
Which they very much preferred.

They crossed the Sound quite quickly,
And, as they approached the land,
They heard a sound that filled their hearts,
It was a Haggis band.

The difference was they were all girls,
The men soon spotted that,
When they saw that gorgeous curls,
Escaped from 'neath each hat.

The men were in a quandary,
And found it hard to choose,
Between the ones who wore the kilts,
And those who wore the trews.

The Haggis Chieftain greeted them,
With a loud 'Och Aye!
Do you come from over there,
Or do you come from Skye?'

They asked him why the band were girls.
He said the men were out
Angling in a nearby loch,
Fishing there for trout.

The visitors were treated well,
And taken to a ceilidh,
In Aros Hall, just on the front,
Decorated gaily.

They danced all day, they danced all night,
With increasing fervour,
Until the girls said 'You're all right,
But we will go no further.'

The Ardnamurchan Chieftain then
Gave thanks with due affection,
He said he'd take back all his men,
The wind had changed direction.

The Angling Haggis came back home
Surprised to see their sisters,
Taking themselves off to bed,
Nursing great big blisters.

The Haggis girls kept to themselves,
The doings of that visit.
They felt it best to cover up
And not be too explicit.

The Angling Haggis puzzled long
About those many blisters,
And never knew what fun was had
By all those spinster sisters!

The Haggis and Burns' Night

On twenty sixth of January
In each and every year,
Every Haggis in the land
Will wipe away a tear.

For on that day, the Haggis say,
They never must forget,
Those who died the day before
On every Burns' night yet.

When Scottish human beings point
To dead on Flodden Field,
The Haggis have an argument
On which they never yield.

Bemoan the dead of Flodden Field,
They say, that is your right,
But how would humans like it
If they were a dish that night?

To feed the craggy kilted folk,
Who gather round a table,
To celebrate the verse and prose
Of Burns of fame and fable.

Burns was just an Ayrshire man,
Who farmed like many others,
He tilled the land, he loved the girls,
And sometimes, too, their mothers.

Celebrate Burns if you must,
The Haggis kindly say,
But can't you find another dish
To eat upon that day?

The Haggis are a kindly bunch,
With no wish to fight and feud,
But they will go to any lengths,
To protect their dwindling brood.

They have already taken steps
Towards that very end,
And just before each Hogmanay
It's northwards that they wend.

They go as far as possible,
And settle in the heather,
In Sutherland and Caithness,
Regardless of the weather.

There among the peat bogs
They rest their weary legs,
And spend the time repairing
Or making filibegs.*

So if one wants to celebrate
On Burns' night any year,
One finds the price of Haggis
Has risen and is dear.

*Filibeg - kilt

But please don't blame the butcher,
He cannot help himself,
It's scarcity that causes it,
There's not much on the shelf.

After Burns' night's over
The Haggis all disperse,
Over all the Highlands,
Free from their annual curse.

The Haggis to the Rescue

Have you ever seen a pasty?
A harmless thing you'd think,
Until you know the story
That they're fiercer than a mink.

Pasties came from Cornwall,
In the dim and distant past.
They bred in bakers' ovens,
And were tame from first to last.

But on one wet and windy day,
On gloomy Bodmin Moor,
A baker's cart became en-bogged
And from the cart's back door,

A family of pasties flew,
A mum, a dad and child,
Who settled underneath a stone,
Because the storm was wild.

And from this little family
One learns and understands,
There grew on misty Bodmin Moor,
The Cornish pasty bands.

No longer tame, they roamed about,
Midst marsh and plain and tors.
They terrified the populace
Who locked themselves indoors.

They terrified the smugglers,
They terrified the elves,
In fact they were so terrible,
They terrified themselves.

If local folk went on a prowl,
Across dark Bodmin Moor,
They listened for the pasty howl,
And feared the pasty spoor.

The age when wicked pasties ruled,
Is 'membered far and wide,
And ended to all men's relief,
At the battle of Pastycide.

The tale of Cornish troubles
Went as far as John o' Groats,
Where friendly Scottish Haggis met
To talk and sail their boats.

The Haggis all decided
That Bodmin should enjoy,
The happiness of Scottish moors,
And said they would employ,

The largest army they could find,
'twixt Sutherland and Peebles,
Of Haggis men - and girls as well -
To fight the pasty evils.

The happy band of Haggis troops
Went quickly o'er the border,
And arrived by night on Bodmin Moor,
In perfect battle order.

When daylight dawned, the Haggis yawned,
And pulled themselves together,
They missed the sea, they missed their mums,
And most of all the heather.

The pasties saw the Haggis troops,
But never overawed,
They mustered all their forces,
Their backs to Camelford.

Some were round and some were square,
And some were elongated,
A terrifying fearsome bunch
Not to be underrated.

The Haggis formed into a square,
And rolled towards the pasties,
The Haggis cry 'We boil and fry',
Was heard from lads and lassies.

The battle raged for days and days,
Until one morn it happened,
The Haggis rolled so very fast,
They had each pasty flattened.

The battle field was widely strewn,
With turnips spuds and gravy,
But the Haggis army tidied up,
And crossed the river Tavy.

Now if one goes to see the site
Where Pastycide was fought,
One will not see a monument,
But there's something of that sort.

For if a seeker takes a look
There are pasties well disguised,
The Haggis built them into walls,
And now they're fossilised.

The Haggis and the Highland Games

One hot day in August,
The Haggis roamed at leisure.
When they hadn't much to do
It always was a pleasure.

Coming close to Tomintoul
They thought they heard a whistle,
But then they found some smaller fry
Had settled on a thistle.

On the road to Bridge of Gairn
Lay a message in the heather,
Perhaps it was exciting news,
Or just about the weather.

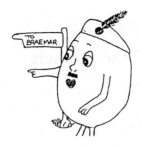

In fact it said that if they went
South westwards on to Braemar,
They'd be in time for Highland Games,
Commencing, two pip emma.

The Haggis all increased their pace
By several rolls an hour,
Getting there for opening time,
In a gentle Scottish shower.

The Chieftain of the Haggis clan
Called, 'Three cheers for the Queen',
Who graciously acknowledged
And said she hadn't seen...

The Chieftain for so many years,
And it would give her pleasure,
If he'd join her for some tea,
If he had the leisure.

The Haggis party followed on
Into the Queen's marquee,
And settled down with great respect,
To take the Royal tea.

The Queen and Chief sat chatting,
Of things plebian and Royal,
While His Highness Prince Philip
Kept the kettle on the boil.

At last the tea was over,
And the Haggis craved to leave,
The Chieftain walking backwards,
Found it quite beyond belief...

That he'd obtained an audience,
Like servants of the Crown,
And despite his motley party,
None had let him down.

The Haggis marched in single file,
As well as they were able,
For some had taken more than tea
At the Royal table!

A crowd of them, but mostly men,
Had sampled malt and beer,
And as a natural consequence
Had tendency to veer.

Across the verdant field they went,
Amid the tossing cabers,
They eyed the men in swinging kilts,
And much admired their labours.

Round and round the field they strode,
Their circle getting smaller,
Just as the Queen came from her tent,
With Philip - he's the taller.

Gazing on the circling crew,
The regal brow was pensive,
She wished the men had stuck to tea,
The malt was quite expensive.

The only cloud that marred that day
Was o'er the Haggis Chieftain,
Who'd hoped the Queen would honour him
With a smart new Haggis tartan.

But when he saw his raucous band
Disrupting every game,
He knew his hopes would come to naught,
And bring upon him shame.

He called his men to order,
And took them all away,
And said he'd give direction
To all of them next day.

The order was as follows:
That Haggis of that Ilk
Commanded that all Haggis men
Should stick to T.T.milk!

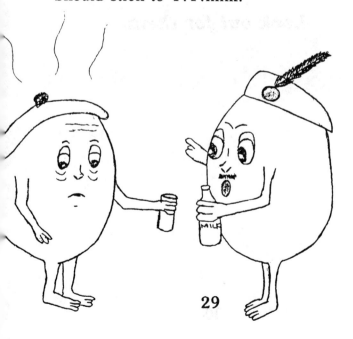

There are more haggis titles around.

Look out for them.